Luke 1:30-31

"Do not be afraid, Mary; you have found favor with God. You will
conceive and give birth to a son, and you are to call him Jesus."

Matthew 1:20-21

An angel of the Lord appeared to him in a dream and said, "Joseph son of David, do not be afraid to take Mary home as your wife, because what is conceived in her is from the Holy Spirit. She will give birth to a son, and you are to give him the name Jesus, because he will save his people from their sins."

Luke 2:4-5

So Joseph also went up from the town of Nazareth in Galilee to Judea, to Bethlehem the town of David, because he belonged to the house and line of David. He went there to register with Mary, who was pledged to be married to him and was expecting a child.

Luke 2:7
There was no guest room available for them.

Luke 2:6-7

While they were there, the time came for the baby to be born, and she gave birth to her firstborn, a son. She wrapped him in cloths and placed him in a manger.

Luke 2:8
There were shepherds living out in the fields nearby…

Luke 2:8
...keeping watch over their flocks at night.

Luke 2:9

An angel of the Lord appeared to the shepherds.

Luke 2:12
"This will be a sign to you: You will find a baby wrapped in cloths and lying in a manger."

Luke 2:13-14

Suddenly a great company of the heavenly host appeared with the angel, praising God and saying, "Glory to God in the highest heaven, and on earth peace to those on whom his favor rests."

Luke 2:15-16

When the angels had left them and gone into heaven, the shepherds said to one another, "Let's go to Bethlehem and see this thing that has happened, which the Lord has told us about." So they hurried off and found Mary and Joseph, and the baby, who was lying in the manger.

Luke 2:19-20

But Mary treasured up all these things and pondered them in her heart. The shepherds returned, glorifying and praising God for all the things they had heard and seen, which were just as they had been told.

Matthew 2:1-2

Magi from the east came to Jerusalem and asked, "Where is the one who has been born king of the Jews? We saw his star when it rose and have come to worship him."

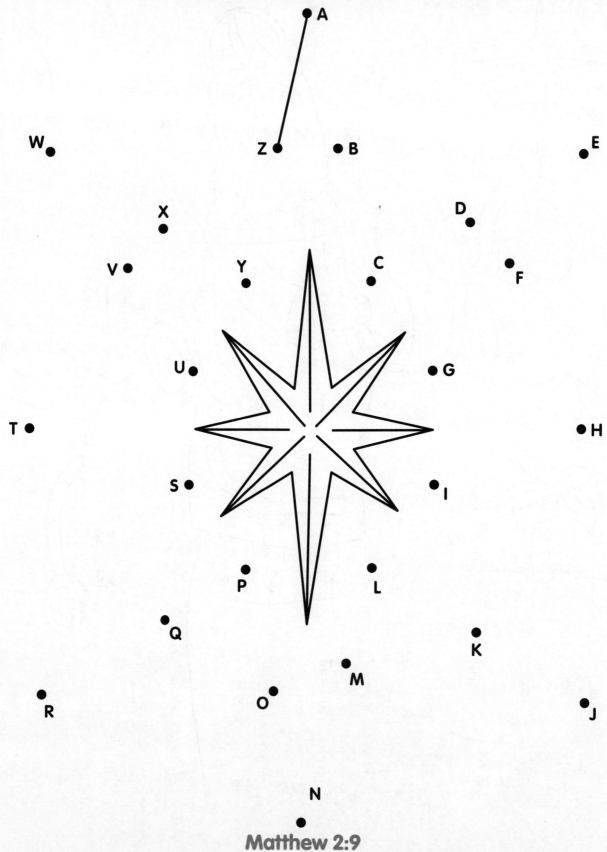

Matthew 2:9

After they had heard the king, they went on their way, and the star they had seen when it rose went ahead of them until it stopped over the place where the child was.

Matthew 2:11

n coming to the house, they saw the child with his mother Mary, and they bowed down and worshiped Him.

Matthew 2:11

Then they opened their treasures and presented him with gifts of gold, frankincense, and myrrh.

Luke 1:37

Use the code below to find out what Gabriel said about God.

"___ ___ ___   ___ ___ ___ ___ ___ ___ ___

___ ___   ___ ___ ___ ___ ___ ___ ___ ___ ___ ___

___ ___ ___ ___   ___ ___ ___."

A	B	C	D	E	F	G	H	I	J	K	L	M

N	O	P	Q	R	S	T	U	V	W	X	Y	Z

Gabriel Visits Mary

Use the code below to find out what the angel Gabriel said to Mary.

"
$\overline{20}$ $\overline{9}$ $\overline{22}$ $\overline{22}$ $\overline{7}$ $\overline{18}$ $\overline{13}$ $\overline{20}$ $\overline{8}$,

$\overline{2}$ $\overline{12}$ $\overline{25}$ $\overline{4}$ $\overline{19}$ $\overline{12}$

$\overline{26}$ $\overline{9}$ $\overline{22}$ $\overline{19}$ $\overline{18}$ $\overline{20}$ $\overline{19}$ $\overline{15}$ $\overline{2}$

$\overline{21}$ $\overline{26}$ $\overline{14}$ $\overline{12}$ $\overline{9}$ $\overline{22}$ $\overline{23}$!

$\overline{7}$ $\overline{19}$ $\overline{22}$ $\overline{15}$ $\overline{12}$ $\overline{9}$ $\overline{23}$

"
$\overline{18}$ $\overline{8}$ $\overline{4}$ $\overline{18}$ $\overline{7}$ $\overline{19}$ $\overline{2}$ $\overline{12}$ $\overline{25}$.

A	B	C	D	E	F	G	H	I	J	K	L	M
26	5	10	23	22	21	20	19	18	11	6	15	3

N	O	P	Q	R	S	T	U	V	W	X	Y	Z
13	12	17	16	9	8	7	25	14	4	1	2	24

Answer: "Greetings, you who are highly favored! The Lord is with you."

Mary Praises God

Use the code below to find out what Mary says. Luke 1:46-47 ICB

,

___ ___ ___ ___ ___ ___
3   2   8   12 25 15

___ ___ ___ ___ ___ ___ ___   ___ ___ ___
17 9   26 18 8   22 8   7   19 22

___ ___ ___ ___ ; ___ ___   ___ ___ ___ ___ ___
15 12 9   23   3   2   19 22 26 9   7

___ ___ ___ ___ ___ ___ ___
18 8   19 26 17 17 2

___ ___ ___ ___ ___ ___ ___   ___ ___ ___   ___ ___
5   22 10 26 25 8   22   20 12 23   18 8

"
___ ___ ___ ___ ___ ___ ___ ___ .
3   2   8   26 14 18 12 9

A	B	C	D	E	F	G	H	I	J	K	L	M
26	5	10	23	22	21	20	19	18	11	6	15	3

N	O	P	Q	R	S	T	U	V	W	X	Y	Z
13	12	17	16	9	8	7	25	14	4	1	2	24

Answer: "My soul praises the Lord; my heart is happy because God is my Savior."

Do Not Be Afraid

```
D R E A M P A R N G E Y V J
O I K U H J A N E O J L N O
N S A V I O R H G L O R Y S
K W H O K I S U A E Y X L E
E I J E S U S T U R L U O P
Y N U N P E K O A D R S V H
A N B N S H E E P R U K E S
F Y L O P N E Q C A L S H I
R Y M A N G E R F A V O R O
A I N A E N O E D P W N S E
I I Q S R B U D N S U K T S
D K B A B Y L A G E D L J J
```

Jesus Is Born!

```
B W R A P P E D N G E Y V D
C E L E B R A T E A I L N B
W E T W G U N T M L M F B T
I W C H R I S T A D Y L T R
S G H B L T H J G R R O A E
E M A N G E R N I A R C N A
M V B N I G H T Z P H K C S
E Y B O R N K E C E M S H U
N Y O X J Z A G M O T H E R
I I N C E N S E O P W K S E
F I R S T B O R N L S S T S
E F W O R S H I P E D L J J
```

CELEBRATE	COWS	BORN	MYRRH
FIRST BORN	CHRIST	BETHLEHEM	WORSHIPED
GIFT	PEOPLE	GOLD	MOTHER
WISE MEN	TREASURES	INCENSE	MAGI
WRAPPED	MANGER	FLOCKS	NIGHT

MINI-BOOK

Instructions

First, read the Bible story from your own Bible.

Next, work together with your child to create "The Best Thing About Christmas" Mini-Book. Help your child color the illustrations on each page, and then cut apart the pages along the dotted lines. The book has 8 pages. Put the pages in order with the cover on top. Staple the pages on the left side to make the book.

Finally, read each page together. Help pre-readers sound out each word, and then discuss the story and its meaning with your child. Encourage your child to think about the story throughout the day and to share thoughts or ask questions.

The Best Thing About Christmas
Luke 2:1-20

1

© 2005 Twin Sisters IP, LLC. All Rights Reserved.

FOLD

One day God sent an angel to Mary. "You will have a baby," said the angel. "He will be the Son of God."

3

FOLD

The shepherds told everyone, "God sent us a Savior."

8

Mary and Joseph named the baby Jesus.

6

Many years ago, God promised to send a Savior.

2

Mary and Joseph traveled to Bethlehem. It was time for the baby to be born.

4

Shepherds came to the stable. They worshipped baby Jesus.

7

There was no room in the inn. The baby was born in a stable.

5

No Room!

FOLD

FOLD

Color the manger, animals, and Bible characters.
Carefully cut along the dotted lines. Glue the manger
together by overlapping the flap until the star forms.
Cut the characters out on the following pages, then
add each to the scene and glue them in place carefully.
Or, set each character in place and retell the story
of Jesus' birth over and over again.